7 KEYS TO ACADEMIC SUCCESS

Ernest Edem Edifor (PhD)

PARTRIDGE

To order additional copies of this book, contact
Toll Free 0800 990 914 (South Africa)
+44 20 3014 3997 (outside South Africa)
orders.africa@partridgepublishing.com

www.partridgepublishing.com/africa

Contents

Dedicated to Jehovah

Education is the most powerful weapon which you can use to change the world.

Nelson Mandela

Knowledge is power. Information is liberating. Education is the premise of progress, in every society, in every family.

Kofi Annan

Preface

Every new beginning comes from some other beginning's end.

Seneca

This book is about how to succeed academically. Academic success is influenced by many factors. However, the biggest of them all is you, the student. In this book, I share my experiences with you and how I believe you can succeed in your academic study. This book is for those who are tired of being losers and hungry to make a tremendous change to their lives, or for those who are doing well but want to do better. There have been several dynamic shifts in my academic life, which have all contributed to my academic success; here are two of them.

When I was in junior high school, a very good friend (now deceased) and I walked to school one morning. On our way, we started talking about the class test we were about to have that day. As we talked, I realised that he was more knowledgeable about the topic than I was. I felt a bit foolish and asked him, 'How do you know these things?' and he said to me, 'They are in our notebooks.' What a shame. While I had watched cartoons, my friend had been reading. This made me feel stupid, but it taught me an important lesson that changed my life: the answers to exam questions are in my notes or textbooks.

The second shift in my academic life was bitter but produced better results. I was very poor in mathematics in my early years. It was my worst subject. I just was not good at numbers. They were too abstract for me even though I was science oriented. My loving mother, who realised I was heading for catastrophe, came to my rescue by asking my father to get me a part-time teacher. His name was Mr Akwei. He was experienced, gentle and very intelligent. He quickly discovered my weaknesses and cooked up a remedy. His principle was that the more exercises you do, the better you get. As the adage goes, 'Anything you do twice becomes easier.' So, he gave me many assignments every week, and his master plan worked. I started getting much better at mathematics, and sooner than I thought, I was one of the best students in mathematics when I got to senior high school, and I loved mathematics. Mr. Akwei was a big part of my success.

The keys to academic success presented in this book are also keys to success in any area of your life; they are life changing. I hope you enjoy this book and, ultimately, find it useful.

Note

We live in a fast-moving world where everybody wants things instantly. Unfortunately, this book is not a quick-learn book but a Do-It-Yourself (DIY) book. You can never learn to play a piano by reading a manual without any practice. You will not derive much benefit from this book if all you do is read it. You need to practise what you learn.

Acknowledgements

No act of kindness, no matter how small, is ever wasted.

Aesop

Thank you Mr & Mrs Edifor:
for being the best parents.

Thank you Mr. Richard Akwei & Dr. Neil Gordon:
for teaching me the way and helping me in my journey.

Thank you Anita:
for being the best and an amazing wife.

Thank you Michelle & Gabriella:
for bringing so much joy into my life.

Thank you Regina, Felix & Sylvia:
for being the most lovely siblings one could ask for.

Thank you Morrison Cloney:
for taking time to edit this book.

Thank you reader:
for reading this book. I hope you find it helpful.

Key 1: Know Who You Are

Knowing yourself is the beginning of all wisdom.

Aristotle

Many people barely exist, thinking of themselves as ordinary human beings living ordinary lives. I have come to realise, unfortunately, that this is the thought pattern of a number of students across the globe. It is a shame that in today's world, most people shy away from accepting challenges because they feel they do not have the potential to do so. This is an unforgivable excuse. Many people throughout history have been able to achieve tremendous and extraordinary results through their hard work and dedication, even those who lived in far less fortunate circumstances.

You are not ordinary. You are unique and filled with enormous potential. You can become whatever you want to become, and do whatever you want to do, if you put your mind to it and work towards your goal. The truth is that you are already a winner. Do you wonder why I say that? You won the most important race of your life before you were conceived in your mother's womb. Research shows that the probability of you being born is very small: one in several million. So, millions of potential human beings competed with you to be borne by your mother, but you won that race against all the odds. You are a winner! You did not win because you were better than other potential human beings were; you won because you were destined to win.

Most people's feeling of being ordinary stems from their environment, their past experience, other people's comments, or their inability to do certain things. If you fall into any of these categories, or some others I haven't mentioned, I want to encourage you now, that you are very special and graciously gifted. There is no one like you, and no one will ever be like you. Your ability to accept how you are and to know that you are not ordinary is a great step towards doing the impossible and achieving success in your academic studies. You don't need to *feel* special. You only need to believe and accept it. It is common knowledge that the way you choose to view things can influence your feelings and potentially affect your performance. See yourself as an achiever, not a loser.

Some people may have physical, financial, mental, emotional or psychological limitations that they feel would hinder them from succeeding in life (in this case academia). I greatly sympathise with anyone in such an unfortunate situation. However, I still believe everyone has the potential to do great things in life. Time and space hinders me from mentioning all who had disabilities but have excelled in their endeavours, including academia. It is believed that Alexander Graham Bell, credited with the invention of the telephone, had learning disabilities. Thomas Edison, who invented the light bulb, picture camera and with many other inventions to his name, had dyslexia and was home-schooled by his mother. Albert Einstein, the most famous physicist of the twentieth century and who proposed the theory of relativity, suffered from a mild form of autism. What is your excuse?

Redefine Failure   *Emotional resilience*

> Failure is simply the opportunity to begin again,
> this time more intelligently.
>
> Henry Ford

What is failure? Your definition of failure can have a tremendous impact on your academic performance. Failure in something doesn't mean you can never succeed in that same area in the future; it only means you have to approach it differently. For example, the fact that a student fails in a mathematics examination does not mean that student can never succeed in mathematics. It only means that the student did not provide the right answer to the set of questions presented in that particular exam and must use a different approach in answering the same question in the future.

Failing in an examination doesn't mean failure in your academic life. You may fail in different things, but you are not a failure until you give up totally. See failure as redirection; it leads you to a better path. Failure just means there is a different and correct way of doing something. Therefore, you have to learn from failure and make better-informed decisions in the future for your success. Your colleagues may laugh at you and/ or tease you for failing in an exam, but you are not a complete failure until you let what they say affect you and eventually give up.

Someone may say, 'Oh, how easy to say that. You've never failed before, so you don't know how it feels to fail.' Well, let me share one of my experiences with you. When I started high school, I decided to get a distinction (grade A) in all my modules, so I worked very hard. My efforts were greatly rewarded in the first few modules I took; I had good passes and scored 70 to 100 per cent in some of my exams. However, during my postgraduate studies, I decided to take a module in learning and teaching in higher education in the UK, since it was my intention to become a lecturer in the future. The exam for this module was an essay (about five thousand words). I wrote the essay to the best of my ability. Unfortunately, the results were disastrous. I scored 40 per cent. I actually had 38 per cent, but the lecturer allowed me some leeway and gave me 40 per cent, so that I might not have to re-sit it.

This was a very big blow, one whose impact I haven't fully recovered from. Disappointed with the result, I booked an appointment with the lecturer for some feedback. I wanted to know where I went wrong so that I could do better. The lecturer's response was simple: I had written the essay from a scientific point of view instead of a social science point of view. But I thought to myself, *I'm a computer scientist, how else was I expected to answer the questions, and how could I have known how to write essays like a social scientist?* It was a bitter experience. From that moment onwards, I decided not to take any more modules. I felt devastated, disappointed, and destroyed. My dreams of getting only distinctions were shattered.

A few months later, I learned about redefining failure. I went on to take another social science module because I wanted to 'fail-forward'; meaning, I wanted to turn my past failures into future success. I did not want to waste my past experience of failure; it taught me a valuable lesson for future success. As you may have rightly guessed, I took other social science modules and excelled in them. This is a simple example of how I tried once, failed, learned from it, tried again and excelled. A famous Chinese philosopher, Confucius, said, 'The greatest glory in living lies not in never falling, but in rising every time we fall.'

Discover Your Purpose

> The will to win, the desire to succeed, the urge to reach your full potential . . . these are the keys that will unlock the door to personal excellence.
>
> Confucius

Purpose, they say, preserves. Anything without a purpose is useless. The book you are reading has a purpose: to challenge you to pursue higher academic excellence. The pen you use, the soap you bathe with, the beating heart in your chest, everything made has a purpose. Therefore, you must know and understand that you are in school for a purpose, and ultimately, there is a purpose for your life. Getting to the highest level in your education should not be the ultimate goal of your life; it should be a means to an end. Your purpose should not be to make millions and nothing more. Your purpose should be to enhance and advance the course of humanity; that's how you'll find true fulfilment. When you know and understand that there is a purpose for your life, you will be careful to live it to its full potential and take your academic studies more seriously. Believe it or not, there is a purpose for your life, and you are in education for a reason. You are here on earth for a specific purpose. You may not know it yet.

No matter what your purpose in life is, you have to do whatever you can, to the best of your ability. It is commonly said that the graveyard is the richest place in the world, because it has most of the untapped abilities. I don't think you will want to exit this planet without living your life to the full. Education or schooling is very instrumental in helping you discover your purpose in life, and it will equip you for that purpose. As a student, you must know and accept this.

Simon Cowell, the producer of a British talent show, once said, 'The secret [to success] is to be useless at school and then get lucky.' Clearly, this is a silly joke and only a handful of people get lucky. Make no mistake, education is very important; it will give you the much-needed foundation you require, no matter what direction you want to follow in life. Nelson Mandela believed 'education is the most powerful weapon which you can use to change the world', and I concur.

Know Yourself

> You are the biggest factor in the determination of
> your fate, be it success or failure.
>
>   Ernest Edifor

It is important for you to know yourself. As mentioned earlier, you are unique, imbued with enormous potential, and you are different from everyone. What works for others may not work for you. Unfortunately, most educational institutions use the same methods to teach all students because it would be extremely costly to develop unique teaching methods to meet each student's individual requirements. For this reason, you must know yourself and discover what works best for you.

Identify your strengths and weaknesses. For example, though I prefer studying in calm environments, I am able to study in busy environments. This means I am able to study in a public area (e.g. on a bus) without being too disturbed. However, some students can only study in calm environments. An example of my weakness is that I cannot study very well at night. If I study very late at night, I feel unwell the next day. On the other hand, some students study best at night. Because I know this is a weakness, I always make the most of my day. Some students study best with visual aids, while others prefer audio aids. Some students are good with numbers, while others are better with words. You must identify your strengths and weaknesses. The remaining chapters of this book will provide tips on how to overcome some common student weaknesses, such as lack of proper organisational skills, procrastination, lack of attention, loss of motivation, etc.

Know your self-worth. As a person, you are very precious. You have the ability to achieve anything you put your mind to and work towards your goal. You have enormous potential. That is why you must not let other people define you. Some students accept the negative things their colleagues, teachers, parents or friends say about them. Never believe the negative things people say about you. You are worth more than that. You can surprise them as many people have done in history. If your teacher says you will never be good at a subject, don't believe it; rather, challenge yourself, and you will surprise them. If anyone calls you dumb-headed, a dunce, or anything similar, don't accept it by believing it. Follow the keys points in this book and you will prove them wrong. Never let others define you; you are the determinant of your fate.

Believing the words of bullies can be dangerous. Some students have ended their lives by committing suicide, because other students said things about them that they did not like. In this modern day, bullying is also widespread on social media (cyber bullying). No matter the form bullying takes (verbal, text, etc.), don't subscribe to it. If you are a bully or you enjoy being in the company of bullies, I would advise you to stop immediately. You don't want to be the cause of someone's unhappiness or even death. If you are being bullied, do not suffer in silence. Seek help from your teacher or qualified counsellor now.

Watch Your Words

> Death and life are in the power of the tongue, and
> those who love it will eat its fruit.
>
> Proverbs 18:21

Don't think I'm being extreme in adding this section about watching your words. I have experienced how your own words can influence you as a student. Words are powerful. If life and death are in the power of the tongue, then you will reap the consequences of your words – whether good or bad.

One evening, while I was an undergraduate student, there was a quiz in a club I belonged to. There were two competing groups, and I belonged to one of them. A few minutes before the quiz was due to end, my team was losing. I had a quick timeout with my team members, and I told them to be confident and that we were going to win. I encouraged them and told them to be positive. Surprisingly, we won the quiz.

If you say positive things to or about yourself, you psych yourself up. It puts your brain and entire body in a ready-to-succeed mode. On the other hand, if you say negative things about yourself, you tell your brain and body to relax because there's 'nothing worth fighting for'. Some students are fond of saying negative things like 'I know I will fail this exam' before even sitting the exam. Some may say, 'I don't think I am going to excel in mathematics, English, history, geography', etc. I would rather challenge you to say things like 'I will pass these exams or subjects if I work hard' and then go on and work hard.

I have to say that positive confessions without using the other key points mentioned in this book can be futile. If you say positive things to yourself and stay positive but don't work hard, remain diligent, avoid procrastination, etc. it doesn't work.

Summary

Knowing who you are is a key to academic success. You are very special and have enormous potential. You have something in you called the 'seed of greatness'; you are the only one who can stop yourself from succeeding.

Failure is not just failing in an exam or in a subject. You will be a failure if you give up entirely on your academic pursuits. Learn from your previous failures, and use those lessons in future endeavours.

Knowing what works best for you, discovering your strengths and weaknesses and acknowledging your self-worth can guard you against self-pity and enable you to achieve academic success.

The more you keep saying something, the more likely you are to see it happen. This is not magic. The more you say something, the more you keep positioning your mind to align with what you say. When your mind aligns with it, your entire being follows. You must watch what you say. Be positive.

Key 2: Train Your Brain

Memory is the mother of all wisdom.

Aeschylus

A student without a good memory is surely doomed to fail; it does not matter what your field of study is, be it sports, music, business or science. As a student, your brain, along with your memory, play an important role in your success. You need your memory to remember things and your brain to think and reason. For this reason, learning to improve your memory by training your brain is essential. Most students do not actively or consciously indulge in training their brains. In fact, most educational institutions do not adequately challenge students to do so. I think this is a big error in those educational systems. Pursuing your education without consciously training your brain and improving your memory regularly is like cutting down a tree with a machete you have not sharpened.

Your brain is the seat of your memory. Your brain is one of the greatest assets you have as a student (and a person). I believe brains are the most intricate and powerful entities in the world. If you are able to train your brain, you will be able to achieve tremendous results. I don't believe there is a single brain that is a complete dunce or dead! Though some students have psychological challenges and mental or learning disabilities, most people do not. Some students' excuse for their poor academic performance is lack of intelligence. This is wrong. I think the most appropriate explanation is their brains are not well trained enough.

The brain works like a muscle; the more you train it, the better it gets. For example, your brain has been trained to read and understand what you're reading now. You could not read this when you were a toddler. Training your brain will take conscious effort and various forms of exercises, just as it does to train your muscles. Your brain loves to be exercised and trusted; it loves to be challenged and trained. In this chapter, I hope to expose you to some techniques (non-exhaustive) that you can use to train your brain. They have been beneficial to me, and I hope you find them helpful.

Be Observant

> Accuracy of observation is the equivalent of accuracy of thinking.
>
> Wallace Stevens

Google is a popular multinational company. I am sure you have heard of it. What are the colours in the Google logo? Can you recollect any of the colours of the characters in the Google logo? Don't feel disappointed in yourself if you cannot remember the colours; I would not be surprised if some of Google's employees failed this test.

For those who have been on the Google website but have failed this test, the reason isn't because you aren't intelligent – this has nothing to do with intelligence – it is because you have not observed the logo keenly; you have not paid attention to its colouring detail. Observation is very important. You can only observe when you are attentive. Most people do not pay particular attention to things they see, hear, feel, etc. They observe things casually, ignoring very specific details.

There's a popular joke on the internet about some freshmen at a medical school who went to their first anatomy class. Upon entering the theatre and gathering round the operating table, they quickly realised they were standing round a human corpse turned face down. A professor came in and began the lesson by telling the students, 'A good doctor must possess two very important qualities. The first is that you must not be disgusted by anything about the human body — dead or alive.' The professor then stuck his finger into the anus of the corpse and then sucked his finger. He instructed the students to do the same. The students could not believe what they'd been told to do. After hesitating for a while, they took turns to stick a finger into the anus of the corpse and then sucked it. When they had finished, the professor told them, 'The second very important quality of a good doctor is observation. I stuck my middle finger into the corpse's anus but then sucked my index finger. You need to pay attention.' This is a joke that I've paraphrased, but it has some valuable lessons.

Observation is the act of monitoring or noticing things, while *attention* is more concerned with focusing (mentally) on things. In the *Oxford Dictionary*, both words are similar and have the word *notice* in their definitions. When you pay attention to things, you observe/notice them. Your ability to pay attention is a great skill that can help you avoid making mistakes in life, even outside the boundaries of schooling. Since it is a skill, it needs to be learned, and this involves conscious training of your brain to stay focused and attentive. It must be noted that your ability to pay attention can be influenced by the environment you are in (noise, moving objects, etc.) or the state you are in (stressed, tired, etc.).

The problem is this: though your brain can allow you to multitask, it usually prioritises the tasks, and it channels most of its resources—focus—onto one of the tasks. The task with the most focus is the task with the most attention. Your brain usually focuses and gives more attention to what you are most interested in. For example, if your teacher is teaching you something about a subject you are not very interested in and there are students making a noise outside, the chances are that you will be listening to the noise coming from outside. However, if your teacher is showing a video that you are very interested in and there are students making a noise outside, the chances are that you will give more attention to the video.

There are various ways of boosting attention/observation skills. The following are some recommendations:

Use FOOT. This is a technique I have developed myself called the Features of Objects Observation Technique (FOOT). It involves identifying the features of a specific object (say, a picture, art, person, device, etc.) and writing down the features in bullet points or lists. This must be done within a specific time, say five minutes. You then pause for some time, say ten minutes, and then start the process all over again but, this time, listing features you did not discover earlier. You continue the process until you can no longer discover any more new features. You have to ensure that all the features you identify are directly related to the object, otherwise your mind will start to wander.

Let's take the logo (below) of my charity as an example.

DEMFA
FOUNDATION

Now, in five minutes, list all the features you observe in the logo above in bullet points.

Did you notice the following?

- The two lines in the middle of *M* form a V shape: a handle for the torch.
- The letter *F* in *foundation* does not start directly beneath the letter *D* in DEMFA.
- The images in the light of the torch are *d* and *f* disguised.
- DEMFA is bigger than *foundation*.

The list could go on and on. One may even list the most repeated character(s), the colour of the logo, the typeface, etc. You could do this with a friend as a competition to see who could come up with the most features within a specific timeframe.

Meditate. Meditation is simply an act of focusing your mind on something and thinking deeply about it in a calm manner. It has been proven that meditating ten to twenty minutes a day can significantly improve one's attention span. You do not have to start with ten minutes a day; you can start with five minutes a day. Once you have mastered that, you can move onto eight minutes then ten minutes. There are many ways of meditating, and various resources (books, websites, etc.) have been dedicated to this topic because of its usefulness.

I am going to share with you three ways in which I meditate personally, but I will suggest that you explore other techniques to discover what works best for you. I love nature and watch so many documentaries on nature: aquatic, arboreal, extra-terrestrial, etc. I usually meditate on these documentaries after watching them. I do so by spending some quiet time, thinking deeply about what I have watched. I also listen to calm meditation songs or instrumentals and think deeply about the wonders of nature. Lastly, I meditate on verses in the Christian Bible. I spend time contemplating on the verses to see their deeper meanings with the help of the Holy Spirit. I must advise you that when you're meditating, you may find your mind wandering and shifting focus. When this happens, don't think that you have failed; just refocus immediately and continue with your meditation.

Do puzzles. Some puzzles can significantly improve your ability to observe. They train your mind to pay attention to details. A classic example is spot-the-difference puzzles, where you have two images where one is missing some details, and you have to identify those missing details. Other interesting puzzles include Memory Match, One of These Things and Find It. There are so many examples on the internet. They are not only fun to do but can significantly improve your attention.

Get curious. Curiosity, they say, killed the cat. Though this has some elements of truth, it is targeted more towards unnecessary inquisition. Curiosity is great if used correctly. Charles Darwin, a world-renowned, nineteenth-century British naturalist, was known for his extraordinary curiosity and attention to detail. Curiosity enables you to obtain in-depth knowledge about something. To get curious, you have to keep asking the questions what, why, who, etc. This will keep your attention on a particular subject and improve your observation. You have to be careful you don't wander away when asking the questions; they should be focused directly on the subject matter.

Live in the moment. Imagine yourself sitting in a car that is speeding. The faster the car, the less attention you have on the environment outside the car, and the less observation you can make. We live in a speedy, hurried world where everything is moving fast. Some students are always in a hurry to complete their classes, so their minds are in a state of inactivity towards the end of the lesson. I have realised that most students are in a hurry to leave examination rooms/centres. They whiz through the questions, provide some answers, and off they go. The funny thing is that they usually don't do anything tangible after that. As it is commonly said, to be attentive you must ruthlessly eliminate hurry from your life. This takes conscious effort. It will make you enjoy the moment. You need to enjoy everything going on, in and around you. You need to slow down to observe or be attentive.

Learn a skill. Most sports and musical instruments require attention. When you are playing a sport or learning to play an instrument or perhaps developing another skill, such as photography, cooking, learning a new language, etc. you need to stay focused and observant. For example, when you are playing football or running on a basketball court, you rarely daydream. Your attention will usually be on the sport. Learning a skill like photography requires attention to detail. Sewing is another skill that requires attention. Exercising is another great way of improving your attention; it has been shown to benefit the brain and the entire body. Yes, exercise does improve attention.

Organize yourself. Organizing your daily activities and following a routine is a great way to keep your mind focused on things. When you don't have a routine or order in your daily activities, you are less likely to pay attention to the tasks you perform. Always endeavour to have a to-do list and try to stick to it. We will talk more about planning in the next chapter.

Note: Attention Deficit Hyperactivity Disorder (ADHD) is a condition some students have that leaves them with a very short attention span, and they are easily distracted. Such students may usually daydream, become restless and hyperactive or impulsive. If you have been clinically diagnosed with ADHD, there are things you can do to improve your attention span. Inform your teacher or tutor about your condition. Do not sit near students who are disruptive in class. Make sure that where you sit in class shields you from things happening outside the classroom. Try and have short breaks during a long teaching session. When you are given big assignments, break them down into smaller tasks if possible. You can also suggest to your teacher to use more visual aids if possible.

Practise Repetition

> Repetition is the mother of learning, the father of action, which makes it the architect of accomplishment.
>
> Zig Ziglar

Repetition is simply the act of doing something over and over, usually in the same way. It is commonly said that whatever you do twice becomes easier. This is common knowledge. Repetition is one of the oldest techniques people have used to enable their brains to get used to something. Aristotle, an ancient Greek philosopher, said, 'It is frequent repetition that produces a natural tendency.'

Do you know why most people can recite the twenty-six characters of the alphabet (A, B, C . . . Z) with ease? It is because they have repeated it endlessly. Think about this: many people can recite the national anthem, the Lord's Prayer and sing nursery rhymes (such as 'twinkle, twinkle little star') because they have had to recite them over and over. It does not matter whether you are intelligent or not. Once you recite them repeatedly, you are bound to recite them by heart.

Though ancient, repetition is one of the most powerful techniques that you can use to train your brain. Whenever you do something for the first time, your brain forms what is called a neural path. This path gets stronger and stronger with repetition. When you have repeated it continuously, you reach a certain point when your brain is able to do it subconsciously. This is why some people can recite nursery rhymes without consciously thinking about it; their minds may be on totally different things while they recite it.

Repetition is extremely powerful and there are no alternative techniques, simply repeat something again and again. Nonetheless, I will suggest that it is easier for most people to repeat something by rhyming. You can rhyme with tunes you are already familiar with. This takes us to our next brain-training technique — association.

Practise Association

> Like readily consorts with like.
>
> Marcus T. Cicero

What mental picture does the word *thirst* paint in your mind? I bet you thought of a drink (water, soda, etc.). If you did, your brain just employed a natural technique it uses in recollecting things. Association is the way the brain uses something it already knows about to remember something it doesn't know. It does this by using something they have in common. So for example, if I meet someone called Vincent, I immediately associate that person with my father, who is also called Vincent. If I meet the person again and want to remember his name, all I have to do is to remember my father's name.

Though the brain naturally uses association in some ways, you can consciously train the brain to use association in a number of other ways to significantly improve your academic scores. Most people use association in remembering names, dates, numbers and lists of things. All they have to do is to associate what they don't know with what they know, and it works like magic.

Sometimes you may not be able to associate easily. If you can't find anything to associate new things with, you can create an absurd association. This is very powerful. Now, let me demonstrate this to you. Carefully examine the list of sixteen objects I have listed below.

car	book	apple	shoe
pencil	knife	table	computer
towel	dog	phone	bed
sugar	sunglasses	mouse	trumpet

If I ask you to look at the above list for five minutes and recollect all the objects from memory, unless you have a photographic memory or you are some kind of genius, you may not be able to recollect all of them. However, you can use the association technique to remember the entire list in no time. Yes, you. You can do it. Let's give it a try.

You will quickly recognize that all sixteen objects in the list are random and do not directly have anything in common. To use the association method, you have to link all the objects by associating them in absurd ways. For example, you can create an association of the objects like this:

There is a car. The car is driven by a book. An apple is crossing the road on which the book is driving. To prevent the apple from being crushed, a shoe comes from nowhere and kicks the apple. The shoe is worn by a pencil. The pencil has a knife. The knife has four legs like a table. On top of the knife-like table is a computer. The computer is covered in a towel. A dog comes to remove the towel. The dog has a phone that rings. The dog's phone is in the shape of a bed. On the phone-shaped bed is someone made of sugar. The person made of sugar is wearing sunglasses. A mouse comes and steals the sunglasses. The tail of the mouse is a trumpet.

The above association is very simple and absurd, but very powerful. It can help you remember all sixteen items with ease. You have to be able to see the story in your mind's eye. This is as simple as it can be. All you have to do is to remember the first object: car. The remaining objects automatically add on with very little mental effort. Try forming your own association from the list and see if you can recollect the objects.

Another way of recollecting all objects in the list is by singing them to a rhyming tune you already know. For example, we are going to use the tune of 'twinkle, twinkle little star' to sing all the objects.

> Car and book and apple and shoe
> Pencil, knife, table, computer
> Towel, dog, phone, and bed
> Sugar, sunglasses, mouse, trumpet

You may have to employ some use of repetition to be able to sing this from memory. However, the use of the 'twinkle, twinkle little star' tune will help you remember the sixteen objects with relative ease.

Association, therefore, helps in both learning and recalling. What a great tool to help train your brain!

Divide and Conquer

> Nothing is particularly hard if you divide it into small jobs.

> Henry Ford

Spotted hyenas are carnivorous animals, which live in sub-Saharan Africa. These hyenas hunt by separating younger animals from their parents and preying on them. Though their prey may be bigger and more powerful than them, their divide-and-conquer technique usually puts them in a winning position.

Divide and conquer simply means breaking bigger tasks into smaller, manageable tasks. It is also another ancient technique employed in politics and the military, and frankly in almost every area in our lives. When you want to go from one end of your classroom to the other end, you don't do it in one leap; you usually take some steps. When you are served a delicious meal, you don't eat the entire dish in one go; you eat it in manageable chunks. You *divide* the food, and you *conquer* the food. Divide and conquer is also known as 'chunking'.

Divide and conquer is not strictly a brain-training technique but it does facilitates them. For example, if you want to learn a song by repetition, you learn it line by line then stanza by stanza. Let's take another example: the speed of light is 299,792,458 metres per second. This nine-digit number is easier to commit to memory if it is broken down into three triple digits: 299 792 458. Always try to break things down into manageable bits. This makes daunting and challenging tasks easier.

I was once invited for a job interview. It was a high-profile company, and they wanted the best candidates. As part of the interview process, I was supposed to take a test. When I looked at the questions, I regretted going for the interview because the questions were difficult, and I thought I was going to look stupid, failing the test even though I had a PhD. However, I decided I would rather try and fail than not try (one of my principles in life). I started dividing the questions into understandable bits, and to my surprise, I was able to conquer them. I couldn't believe it. I was so proud and glad to hand the answers back. What a great advantage the technique of divide and conquer gave me. It is a vital lesson I will never forget.

Next time you are introduced to a topic that you don't understand, or are attempting to sit a difficult examination question, try using divide and conquer. Divide the topic or question into manageable chunks and conquer it. I understand you may not be able to divide and conquer everything all the time, but at least use the technique when appropriate, and you will not regret it.

Other Memory Techniques

The following are some tips (that I have not mentioned) that will help your ability to memorize things. You have to experiment with them and identify what works best for you.

Acronym. An acronym is a set of letters one uses to represent the first letter of a sentence, phrase, etc. For example, most people use ROY G. BIV (as somebody's name) to remember the colours of the rainbow: red, orange, yellow, green, blue, indigo and violet.

I use acronyms a lot. I use them in remembering definitions, Bible verses, phrases, etc. The *Oxford Dictionary* defines *light* as 'the natural agent that stimulates sight and makes things visible'. If I am to memorise this definition using acronyms, I would use something like NASS TV (natural agent stimulate sight things visible). This does not contain all the words in the definition, but at least it will serve as a mental catalyst for remembering the entire definition. As you can see, I have no letter for the word *makes* in the acronym. This is because if I replace the word *makes* with a synonym, it will not change the meaning of the definition.

Acronyms may not be easy to form for most things, but if you train yourself to employ them, they will prove useful. Going back to the Google logo I mentioned earlier, the colours of the letters are blue for *G*, red for the first *o*, yellow for the second *o*, blue for *g*, green for *l*, and red for *e*. If you find memorizing colours as difficult as I do, you will use BRY BGR (which in my mind sounds like a shortcut for *bry burger*).

Mnemonics. Mnemonics are words, sentences, phrases, or a pattern or combinations of letters and numbers that help you to memorize and recollect information. Mnemonics are usually simple but very effective. There are so many examples of mnemonics on the internet that you can use in your studies.

Mnemonics can be used in helping you remember how to spell words correctly. For example, 'A rat in the house may eat the ice cream' is commonly used to help spell ARITHMETIC.

They can also help you distinguish between the spellings of words that are confusing for some people. For example, some students struggle to spell the word *lie* or *believe*. You can use the following: 'Learning is exciting [LIE]; never believe in a lie.' Others would rather use another common saying: '*I* before *E*, except after *C* or when the word sounds like *neighbour* or *weight*'. Meaning, any time *I* and *E* are together, always use *I* before *E* except when they come after *C* (such as in *receive*) or they sound like *neighbour* or *weight*. Beware: there are still exceptions to this rule for words such as *weird*.

You can also use mnemonics to differentiate meanings. The words *desert* and *dessert* confuse many people. The former refers to a dry, desolate land with no vegetation, while the latter refers to sweet treats after meals. All you have to know is that the spelling with *ss* is the one with more sugar.

Another common use of mnemonics is in memorizing and recollecting the order of things. For example, in biology, some students use 'Kids prefer cheese over fried green spinach' to remember kingdom, phylum, class, order, family, genus and species. Another common example is the use of 'Every good boy deserves favour' to remember musical notes representing lines on the treble clef stave.

Sleep induced. I was in a boarding school during my high school days. 'Mining' (as if we dug some precious metals) was a term we used to describe the time we spent burning the midnight oil. I remember how, during mining, I could repeat things I had previously memorised to myself when I awoke in the morning. 'Mining' employs the use of some of the techniques I have talked about previously, such as repetition and chunking etc. However, the advantage of this method is the inclusion of the process of sleep. I have never been a good 'miner' because I am not able to study at night. However, the few times I have memorised things before sleeping, I realise that I am able to recall them easily. It is said that this technique helps you remember just about anything you've previously memorised: dates, text, numbers, and sequences etc.

Sharing with others. When I was in high school, my best friend (who is my pastor now), Rev. Clifford G. Kasim, used to tell me about the topics he had learned in class. Initially, I found it absurd because he was a visual arts student, and I was a science student. However, I learned a very valuable lesson from that. Whenever he shared what he had learned with me, he reinforced the information into his memory. Whenever he got stuck (that is, he could not remember something), he went back to his notes to remind himself. This works like repetition but has a twist. Sharing with someone is more interesting than repetition to oneself. It also helps you remember things easily.

Most evenings, before my kids go to bed, I ask them to tell me what they've done that day. I consciously do this to help them develop their memory in recollecting things. When they share that information with me, they force their brains to remember. Share what you learn with your friends, parents, study group, etc. and you'll be surprised at the results. If you don't have anyone to share with, go and stand in front of the mirror and talk to yourself. This technique works for both theoretical and practical subjects. Try it today.

There are many more techniques available for improving your memory. Most of these techniques use combinations of those mentioned above, especially repetition, chunking, and association. Sample exercises on these techniques are freely available on the internet; explore them.

Seek Understanding

> And with all thy getting get understanding.
>
> Proverbs 4:7

There is a big difference between knowing something and understanding what it is. You may know something, but that does not mean you understand it. Knowledge is basically the keeping of facts, information, principles, etc. in mind. If you ask me what my name is, I will tell you Ernest (traditionally spelt Earnest). Why? Because I know that Ernest is my name: my parents told me; I have seen it on my passport, certificates, etc. It is also through knowledge that I know that Ernest means 'serious'. Understanding, however, is the extraction of meaning from what you know (knowledge). The fact that I know my name is Ernest does not mean I understand what it means to have the name of Ernest. It is through understanding that I will respond to everyone who calls me by the name Ernest because I know it is my name, and I understand that my name is what people call me by.

You may know that 1 + 1 = 2, and you may also know that 2 + 2 = 4, but if you don't understand how the addition operator works, you may struggle to know what 23 + 89 will yield. Some students may know that in biology, the term *metamorphosis* is used to describe how a caterpillar becomes a butterfly. However, not all students may understand the process of metamorphosis (which is a Greek word for *transform*). When you understand the way something fundamentally operates, you are less likely to forget it.

Let's consider another practical example to clarify this point. You've just been taught by your tutor that rocks are grouped into three categories: sedimentary, metamorphic and igneous. If you don't pay attention to understand how these rocks are formed, you may know the names of these rocks, but you will miss the more important lesson on how they're formed. Albert Einstein said, 'Any fool can know. The point is to understand.' It may take a minute to know something, but it can take a lifetime to understand it. The Bible did not mince words when it said 'With all thy getting get understanding.' The New International Version says, 'Though it cost all you have, get understanding.' Understanding is key; if you can understand a principle, you will be more likely to be able to apply it to most problems within its domain.

I understand that in certain circumstances, one may not be able to attain full understanding of what he or she is being taught.

For example, if you're studying a very difficult, abstract concept like calculus, you may not fully understand it. Worst of all, if your tutor/lecturer is not skilled in transferring knowledge, the subject becomes a dreadful nightmare. In these circumstances, I would advise you to read more resources on the subject/topic for a better understanding. You may also contact a colleague or tutor who can enlighten you further. Unless it is absolutely necessary to leave, I would advise you to stay in a boring teacher/lecturer's class because if you pay enough attention, you will learn something from the class no matter how boring it is.

For practical students whose field of study require hands-on practices, the best way to understand things may be by doing them. Confucius rightly said, 'I hear and I forget. I see and I remember. I do and I understand.' I studied computer science right from undergraduate level to PhD level. I know only too well that any student (new to coding) who does not continuously code will surely not be able to understand coding. They may read about it, commit syntaxes to memory, etc. but they need to practise before they can fully understand and appreciate the coding. This is true for many similar fields.

I would advise you to always pursue understanding. When you understand things, you are more likely to remember them and spend relatively less time on revising them.

Summary

> Whatever any man does he first must do in his mind, whose machinery is the brain. The mind can do only what the brain is equipped to do, and so man must find out what kind of brain he has before he can understand his own behaviour.
>
> Gay G. Luce and Julius Segal

Your brain is one of the most important assets you have as a student. Training your brain is a necessary part of your academic excellence and an important skill for future success. You can train your brain to be observant. You can improve your memory by repetition, association, chunking, etc.

Another crucial skill you need is the pursuit of understanding. I strongly recommend that, if possible, you seek understanding in the subjects or topics you are taught. This may require further reading outside the curriculum or asking other knowledgeable people.

Key 3: Plan Your Time

Failing to plan is planning to fail.

Alan Lakein

Knowing who you are is insightful, and improving your memory is helpful. However, if you are not able to plan your time, you will most likely waste it. If you cannot plan one day of your student life, it is very likely you cannot plan one term, semester, or trimester. Since your academic success is hidden in your daily routine, your ability to take control over your day can have a significant impact on your final results.

Apart from your memory, another important asset to any student (in fact, every human being) is time. Time is priceless. Time is precious. It is a non-renewable gift; once it is spent, it cannot be reused. Everyone has equal amounts of time in a day: twenty-four hours. How you spend yours will determine your level of success. You have to learn to respect time. I concur with Charles Darwin when he said, 'A man who dares to waste one hour of time has not discovered the value of life.'

What would happen if you're one hour late for your exam? In most institutions, you will never be allowed to sit an exam if you're more than thirty minutes late. What would happen if you skip classes/lectures to do something completely irrelevant? You may miss very important information passed on during the class/ lecture. What would happen if you waste some of your time? You are actually wasting some of your life.

As a student (or a person), you must have great respect for time, because your life is expressed in this world in terms of time. Therefore, one can say time is life. That is why I strongly agree with Charles Darwin's quote that you don't know the value of life if you waste one hour. Your respect for time will enable you to live a purpose-driven life.

Plan Today

> The clock is running. Make the most of today. Time waits for no man. Yesterday is history. Tomorrow is a mystery. Today is a gift. That's why it is called the present.
>
> Alice M. Earlet

Yesterday is gone. Time spent can never be retrieved. Tomorrow, really, never comes. All you've got is today. The way you spend today can significantly impact your future. Planning your 'today' is a great way of securing future success.

I read a book some time ago that talked about viewing time (twenty-four hours) as currency that you have to spend in a shop called Today. To paraphrase the analogy, consider yourself going shopping with only twenty-four hours (time is the currency) available to get everything you want. The items in the shop are the things you would want to do, like studying, going for classes, sleeping, watching TV, eating, etc. How are you going to spend your twenty-four hours? Common sense and experience will tell you that without planning, you may impulse-buy and spend the money (time) on things you may want without buying very essential things you really need. A great way to avoid this pitfall is to have a plan and stick to it. If you know the items you really need, you go for them first, and if you have some spare time, you go for the things you want.

This means, to be productive in a day, you must have a plan for that day. You must know what you really need to commit your time to and when to actually do it. After that, if you have some spare time, you can do the things you want. If you don't have a plan, you just follow anything that comes your way, and you are most likely to lose control of your life. Below are some steps I would recommend to help you plan your day:

1. Choose an appropriate time to plan your day; it could be every morning or the night before. From my experience, the latter suits most people.

2. Write down the things you have to do during the day. These must include things you couldn't do the day before and things you need or want to do on the day you're planning for.

3. Prioritise the tasks by grouping them under those that are immediate and/or important. Make sure the immediate

and important ones are first, then important ones and then finally the unimportant ones.

4. If possible, allocate times to these tasks. This will help you not to waste any time.

5. Review your plan and make sure it is feasible and reasonable.

Below is sample plan:

5 a.m.–6 a.m.: Prayer and devotion
7 a.m.–8 a.m.: Breakfast/ready for classes
8.30 a.m.–12.30 p.m.: classes (maths, biology)
12.30 p.m.–2 p.m.: break
      - post letter, speak to Mr Tom
2 p.m.–5 p.m.: classes (English, chemistry)
5 p.m.–7.30 p.m.: shower/dinner
7.30 p.m.–9 p.m.: homework/ study
      - revise for maths exams

I used to carry a to-do list every day, and would highly recommend it, because it has proven to be extremely useful. When you are able to work through your plan, you derive a great sense of achievement from each day. Apart from the joy of achievement it provides, you are also able to keep track of tasks and stay up to date with your responsibilities.

You don't have to be rigid with your plan. Though you have to jealously guard it against time wasters, you have to be flexible enough to allow unexpected events. As you can see from the sample to-do list, I may have some spare time (flexible) between

7 a.m. and 8 a.m. and between 5 p.m. and 7.30 p.m. Sometimes, some things may happen to completely thwart your plan. For example, using the plan above, let's assume at 12 noon, during the biology class, a colleague collapses, and I have to take him home. Let's say because of this incident, I miss the break period and also part of the English period. For most people, this will destabilize them for the rest of the day, but that doesn't need to happen. After taking my sick colleague home, I will go for a quick break, join the English lesson, and continue with the remaining items on the plan as normal. If I have some spare time between 5 p.m. and 7.30 p.m., I will post the letter and speak to Mr Tom. If I don't have any spare time, I will postpone these to the next day.

Sometimes, the interference with your plan will cause you to reschedule your plan entirely. For example, using my to-do list above, if the English lesson is cancelled for one reason or other, I may revise for my maths exams during that session and do something else in the evening. At other times, you may have to entirely abort the plan, if for example, you're sick. No matter what happens, the secret to success in handling thwarted plans is to be resilient and always reschedule as soon as possible.

Finally, let me inform you that if you're not used to planning your day, you may fail during the initial stages and not be able to stick to the plan. This is normal. Good planning is a skill, and you will have to develop it. If you fail, don't worry; just keep on trying. Do it over and over until you are able to master it.

Planning is a great skill to have for life, because failing to plan is planning to fail.

Avoid Procrastination

> My advice is to never do tomorrow what you can do today. Procrastination is the thief of time.
>
> Charles Dickens

According to the *Oxford Dictionary*, *procrastinate* and *postpone* may mean the same thing: to delay or put off doing something. In this book, I make a slight distinction between the two. *Procrastination* is delaying what you *can* do today or right now for a later time, while *postponing* is delaying what you *cannot* do today or right now for a later time. Therefore, I'm making *postponing* a good thing and *procrastination* a bad thing.

If you have the ability to do something today or right now, please never put it off for a later time. You may never have the time to do it later. Procrastination can bring many regrets. One of my big regrets is achieving a 69.09 aggregate score in my master's degree when I could have easily scored over 70.00. This is because I did not do very well in one of my exams. The night before that exam, I was revising when a friend approached me to help him with a problem on his computer. I foolishly put off my studies and attended to his computer. Unfortunately, I could not then revise properly before the exam because I could not make up the time later on. The most painful aspect of this foolish act was that the questions I could not answer in the exams were exactly what I was looking at when this friend approached me for help. Don't procrastinate if at all possible.

Avoid Distraction

> By prevailing over all obstacles and distractions, one may unfailingly arrive at his chosen goal or destination.
>
> Christopher Columbus

The experience I've just shared shows that I procrastinated for a seemingly just cause, but it was not worth it in the end. Most of us procrastinate for very flimsy, pointless reasons. These are what we call distractions or time-wasters. Distraction may not necessarily be a substitute for things we delay doing, but they can surely have equally devastating effects. For this reason, I would advise you to vehemently resist them.

Distraction may happen subtly in the classroom when a colleague draws your attention away from what is being taught. It may also happen in the exam hall; I'm sure you're familiar with this. It may also happen when you're learning or revising. No matter which form it takes, you have to be able to identify it and avoid it. Sometimes, you will need to be wise and/or strong-willed to do this.

I believe today's students live in an era where there are more distractions/time-wasters than ever before. Technological gadgets that promote internet surfing, gaming, chatting, gossip, etc. have become ubiquitous at most educational levels today, all over the world. Though technology in itself is a great tool to enhance learning, it can also become a student's biggest distraction if you are not careful. I am not going to leave you helpless. Below are some tips on how to avoid distractions. These tips also help you avoid procrastination too.

Plan and prioritise. It is commonly said that if you don't know where you're going, any road will lead you there. This is true for planning. If you don't have a plan that is properly prioritised, you may end up doing anything that comes your way. If you plan and prioritise your day, you can easily escape distracting traps.

Follow the plan. Once you have a plan, you must follow the plan. Having a plan is easy; following a plan may prove more challenging. It takes discipline to follow a plan, and you must follow it tenaciously. If you are in high school or university, you may receive a call, text, email, etc. that can distract you. You must include such social media in your plan if necessary. For example, you must have specific times for checking your email, texts, messages, etc. When I was a postgraduate student, I usually checked my emails and browsed the internet at specific times of the day, usually after doing some meaningful work. If you don't plan for such events, you will end up getting distracted by them.

*Say **no** when necessary.* Don't be afraid to say no when necessary. I have told you of how I foolishly decided to work on a friend's computer at the expense of my studies. I should have said no at that instant and told him to come back after the exams. That was the most logical thing to do. Sometimes, you have to say no to distractions or postpone them. Never procrastinate dealing with items on your plan; procrastinate dealing with distractions.

I remember one evening during my undergraduate study, after an unproductive group meeting, my colleagues and I decided to retire to our hostels. On the way, I felt a strong urge to go back to the library to study. I fought this feeling because I didn't want my colleagues to think I was being too serious with my studies, and they were good company. I finally decided to go back to the library to do some further studies. To my surprise, all the material that I revised that evening in the library were the exact answers to most of the questions asked in the exams the next day.

Avoid drifting off. Sometimes while studying or revising, you may find yourselves drifting off by doing something unrelated to the study. For example, when searching for information online or in a library, you may find yourself drifting off unto other unrelated websites or books. One great key to help you stay focused in such situations is to have a search list or a study guide. When you find yourself drifting off, quickly get back on track with the search list.

Sometimes students drift off because they are tired or worried about something. If this is the case, I would advise you take some rest (if you're tired) or seek some counselling (if you're worried) and study at an appropriate time when you are more able. Other times, you may drift off while studying long hours. The solution to this is not to procrastinate but to take regular short breaks. Another reason students may drift off while studying is when the subject they're studying is too difficult. In this case, break the topic you're studying into manageable chunks. If chunking doesn't work, consult a colleague who is more knowledgeable than you are. If you don't have a colleague to consult, use the internet (be careful not to drift off) or consult your teacher or lecturer.

Avoid the obvious. Though some distractions are subtle, most are pretty obvious — all you need to identify them is common sense. Avoid conditions, locations and people that/who are potential distractions. I know very well that I cannot study mathematics on my bed; I do it better when I am in a more attentive mood. If staying at home will present distractions, don't stay at home to study with the intention of fighting those distractions. If studying in the library avoids distractions (which is true for most people), then study in the library. If a friend of yours is naturally a distractor, avoid that person when it is time to get serious with studies. You are not being mean to that person; you are instead securing your future.

Watch the relationship trap. Many students have wasted their precious time and resources on people they thought they would marry in the future. From personal experience, I have realised that less than 5 per cent of primary or junior high school pupils in such relationships thrive, and less than 10 per cent of high school lovers end up in meaningful relationships. Most relationships formed in the final year of undergraduate studies or postgraduate studies thrive better. This is just my observation, but I think it is true in most cases. Why would you waste your time and resources on someone who may never be part of your life at the expense of your education? Unhealthy boyfriend/girlfriend relationships are a complete distraction. Beware of this trap. This is my advice: if you are not in the final stages of undergraduate study, focus on your education, and when you're successful, you can look for a partner.

Enjoy Your Day

> The most important thing is to enjoy your life—to be happy—it's all that matters.
>
> Audrey Hepburn

Having the mindset to enjoy your day, instead of enduring it, has a great influence on your ability to plan and follow your plans for the day. Some students have hate-days because they have a difficult subject on that day, or it's a Monday, or they have a test/ exam that day, or something else they hate about that day. Almost everyone has days like that but, surely, you would rather enjoy the day. Life is short; we live it only once, and we live it in days. You might as well enjoy it. When you enjoy your day, it gives you the psychological boost to continue planning and following your plans for the day. However, if you don't enjoy the day, you lose motivation to plan and follow your plans for the day. Here are some keys to help you enjoy every day of your school life.

Be present. Endeavour to be present in classes/lectures as often as you can. If you miss some classes or lectures and you are not able to catch up with the tutor, you are more likely to lose interest in that class. I understand some teachers are boring and students don't like them. I would still advise you to be punctual and present at every lecture whenever possible. Make the day lively if you can.

Be participative. Endeavour to take part in the day's activities. Do not shy away. Asking questions in class can help you have more interest in the lesson and can improve your understanding of the topic. It makes a boring class more interesting too. Sometimes you can confirm what you understand with the tutor by asking questions like, 'Does that mean . . . ?' This helps eliminate any assumptions and clarify any uncertainties. Ask questions even if you think they might be the wrong questions. You're in school to learn; that's what you pay huge sums of money for.

Be prepared. Confucius said, 'Success depends upon previous preparation, and without such preparation there is sure to be failure.' It is always a good thing to go through your day prepared. If you know what you're going to be taught, it is worthwhile to read ahead if possible. If you are going to have some exams or tests on that day, it is common sense that you prepare very well for them. If there are things you will need at school on a particular day (including lunch, homework, tools, etc.), it is expedient to get them packed and ready the previous night. Nobody likes unpleasant surprises, so if you can prevent them, please do so. You will enjoy the day better that way. Having a good night's sleep and a healthy breakfast can also help you prepare physiologically for the day.

Pursue interests. If you have the opportunity to choose your subjects or topics, always go for those you're most interested in. I understand this may not always be feasible, but it will be in some cases. If you don't have the opportunity to choose subjects you're interested in, do not hate those subjects you are not interested in. Rather, always seek to understand the subjects/topics and solve more questions or examples on that subject or topic. This will give you some confidence to help you study it, and it will take away any fear of that subject.

Pamper yourself. After a hard day's work, it is advisable to reward yourself. This can take any form, such as playing games, watching a favourite TV show, going to the movies, going out for a meal (if you have time), spending time with friends, going shopping, using social media, etc. It should be something you enjoy doing. When you reward yourself, forget about your books and enjoy the moment thoroughly. Make sure the time you spend on rewarding yourself is also in your daily plan. Treat yourself when it is deserved.

Summary

Time is another precious asset a student has. If you don't value time, you don't value life. Your ability to plan today can lead to a successful tomorrow. Failing to plan is planning to fail.

Procrastination, as commonly said, is the thief of time. Distractions rob you of the opportunity to do something meaningful. You must learn to avoid both procrastination and distractions; their repercussions can be grave.

You must tune your mind to enjoy every day. Being present, participative, prepared, pursuing interests and pampering yourself can significantly improve your ability to enjoy the day.

Key 4: Work Hard

There is joy in work. There is no happiness except in the realization that we have accomplished something.

Henry Ford

Work is good. Work is natural. Anything that stops working starts dying. If your heart stops working, it will start dying. The most extraordinary human achievements or advancements have been produced by people who worked hard. All successful athletes, musicians, academics, inventors, architects, biologists, theologians, business persons, etc., have succeeded because they have worked hard; hard work is the common denominator in their success.

As Thomas A. Edison, the inventor of the electric light bulb, would say, 'There is no substitute for hard work.' The world has no place or reward for lazy hands. If you entertain laziness, you will not go far in life. Make hard work a principle for your life. Hard work sets you apart; it makes you distinguished. Hard work will make you prosper in your academic endeavours. Hard work is an intrinsic part of my success, and I would like to share some of my experiences with you. I hope they challenge you.

As I shared with you earlier, one of the major shifts that led to my academic success was my mother getting me a part-time, out-of-school teacher. Mr Akwei was a very nice gentleman who gave me lots of assignments after teaching me a topic. The arduous tasks were not meant to break me but to make me. I quickly realised that hard work, usually, does not make you bitter, but better. As I laboured through the tasks, I quickly became better at them. I was a sub-average maths student before meeting Mr Akwei, but after nearly three years of his 'torture', I became the best maths student in my class. I attribute this chiefly to hard work.

Another period of my academic life when I had to put in a great deal of effort was during the first year of my undergraduate study in university. Being a computer science student then, I was introduced to computer programming – a topic I found quite challenging. After the first year, I realised I was really struggling with computer programming and had to do something about it. During the long vacation after the first year (lasting three months), I found an electronic book on computer programming with lots of examples and exercises. I worked through them day and night. I devoured its content like a hungry bear. At the end, it paid off. For my final year project, I used a computer programming language (C#) I learned on my own.

Although I taught myself to programme by working hard, you sometimes need a mentor to challenge you to work hard. I remember during my PhD studies when my principal supervisor introduced me to an undergraduate student who needed some mentoring in computer programming so that he could undertake his final project. For the purpose of confidentiality, I will call this student PM. First I introduced PM to some basic principles in programming with some examples. After that, we wrote a few computer programmes and I assisted him with some of his assignments. I must clarify here that I did not do his assignments for him but explained what was required of him, and he went ahead and did them.

The time came when PM had to write his final-year project. A colleague of his advised him to pay professionals to do the work for him, which he refused. He decided to work on the project himself. PM worked really hard. He had to work day and night, neglecting his much-loved computer games. You will be pleased to know that his hard work paid off. He had an extremely good result in his final-year project. I was so proud of him. Nearly a year after completing his studies, I had the following email (below) from him:

> Hi Ernest
>
> It's PM I don't know if you remember me but you helped me a lot during my undergraduate. I hope you got your Ph.D. and you are teaching. The students would really benefit from your knowledge. I have already started my master degree in Network Security; I couldn't have gotten in without your help getting good grades.
>
> Thank you.
> Sincerely,
> PM

Work Smart

No matter how hard you work, if you are not doing the right things, you will never get the right results. Working hard may not always translate into success. You have to be clever, otherwise you will dissipate your energy on so many unimportant things. Below are some smart-working techniques.

Get up to date. If you miss a class/lecture, make sure you get up to date by ensuring that all your notes, tutorials, etc., are up to date. Sometimes teachers/lecturers give directions on where their students should focus their learning. If you miss such vital information, you may end up spending so much time on unnecessary topics. Make sure you are up to date on everything as much as possible.

Solve past questions. Solving past questions is a huge step in working smart. It introduces you to teachers' or lecturers' styles of questioning. It also gives you the opportunity to have a mock examination. Therefore, if past questions are available, endeavour to go through them all. Ask your tutor if he/she is willing to look over your answers. If they do, they will direct you on how they want questions answered. This is very important because though you may have the answers to certain questions, your approach in answering them may not give you maximum marks.

Be accurate. There is no point in trying to complete an exam or assignment in time if you do not provide accurate answers. Accuracy is preferred over speed. Speed is important, but you must make sure you're accurate. As you work hard on studying your notes, doing your assignments, undertaking tutorials, etc., ensure you have time to do them all accurately; otherwise, your efforts may be futile. Don't be in a hurry to rush out of examination halls or rush to first to finish your assignments or tasks. Always make sure you have provided the right answers.

Prepare for exams. Most students like to do assignments at the last minute or prepare for exams a few weeks/days beforehand. This is surely not a smart way of working. Putting so much pressure on yourself a few minutes before submission is definitely not a healthy and wise thing to do. I have done it before and would not recommend it. This does not mean you should not study during or prior to exams. No, what I recommend is, from day one, to start preparing yourself for exams. If you study more hours during exam periods, that is fine. I remember during my undergraduate study, I used to spend over twelve hours a day studying during examination periods, but I made sure I was answering past questions, studying my notes, etc., several months before that time. I will talk more about preparing for exams in Key 6.

Don't cheat. Most students who cheat are usually those who have not worked hard enough. Integrity is very important. If you cheat, you are not only breaking the law, you may end up nullifying all your efforts and getting other people in trouble. Do not cheat. Avoid cheating in any way, shape, or form.

Just Do it

Your ability to do what is expected of you, regardless of your feelings, is powerful. We, as humans, are all influenced by our feelings in one way or another. However, our ability to overcome our feelings determines the extent of our exploits. Sometimes, our feelings are stirred by our physical state. For example, one may feel genuinely tired, sick or sleepy, but we sometimes feign these feelings when we want to make excuses or we dread taking some actions.

Sometimes students become mentally tired and disinterested when they have to study. For some of these students, it is because they have not fully cultivated the habit of studying and of self-motivation. To overcome such feelings you must seek other sources of motivation, which could be a study partner or study group. One crude way I used to overcome such a false sense of tiredness or weakness was to ignore the feeling. Yes, you have power over your emotions. I usually told myself, 'Feel the feeling, but do it anyway.' You have to be hard on yourself sometimes. I was hard on myself by saying, 'Hey, man, you're going to spend two hours in this library whether you feel like it or not.' Once you precondition your mind to do something, apply yourself to it and you'll achieve it. It has worked for me, and I've learned to overcome other emotions, like anger, impatience, etc. Challenge yourself; ignore the false sense of tiredness, laziness, etc., and work hard on your studies. Just do it!

Reassess Your Work

Rereading reveals rubbish and redundancy.

Duane Alan Hahn

I have realised that most students hurry to get out of the exams halls before the scheduled time of the exams is over, or they rush to complete assignments. This could be because they've provided all the answers to the exams questions or they simply could not. No matter the reason, I would encourage you to stay in the exam hall, examining your work until the examination time has ended. Reassessing your work means going through every single piece of the question asked in an exam or assignment and the corresponding answers you have provided. Reassessing involves checking the work for correct answers, grammar, spelling, accuracy, etc.

Someone may say, 'Oh, I re-examine my work before submission.' Well, I say, keep re-examining your work until the exam period is over and then you submit it. Here are some reasons for saying that:

1. You may end up wasting the time. When you leave the examination hall early, what do you do with the extra time? Some students spend the time waiting for other students (their friends) to finish their exams. Some spend the time going for a meal. Some spend the time playing games, and very few spend the time preparing for the next exams.

2. Reassessing your work could reveal errors. I rarely leave the examination halls before the time allocated for the examination is over for this very reason. I can give countless examples of this from my own academic experience. Sometimes during reassessment, I realise I have misspelt words or calculated wrongly, missed some questions, wrongly labelled answers, misinterpreted questions, etc. Never be too confident of the answers you provide in an exam hall or for an assignment. Overconfidence can be a big impediment to success. When you have completed an exam or assignment and you have more time to spare, put yourself in the shoes of the examiner and assess your work. You will be surprised at the improvements this can make.

3. Handle difficult questions wisely. Some people leave examination halls early because they are unable to answer all the questions. Reassessing your work gives you the opportunity to think over your work meticulously. Someone may say that if you don't know the answer to an exam question, don't waste your time on it. Yes, don't waste your time on difficult questions if you don't have time to spare; focus on the easier questions. However, if you have ample time to spare, why not consider trying to understand the difficult questions? When I was given a test in an interview for a job I applied for some time ago, while I was doing the test, I realised there were a few difficult questions I had no answers to. After providing answers to the easier questions, I turned to the more difficult ones. I read them repeatedly until I was able

to make sense of them. Fortunately for me, the answers were results of simple calculations I could easily perform. Reassessment paid off. I felt really proud of myself that I fought the temptation to give up and reassessed my work. Albert Einstein said, 'It's not that I'm so smart, it's just that I stay with problems longer.'

Make Work Interesting

Though hard work (in this case, studying) is rewarding, it can be uninviting. You need to make studying hard a habit. However, this is not easy to do. If you are not naturally a hard worker, I suggest you start cultivating this habit by making work interesting. You are more likely to enjoy studying when it is interesting to you. Here are some tips on how to make studying interesting.

Use technology. Nowadays, technology has become an integrated part of most educational systems. There are various games, tutorials, documentaries, simulations, models, etc., available in educational institutions or on the internet that may be capable of easing your studies. Don't shy away from these technologies, but rather, use them. If they are not available to you and you have an idea about how technology can make studying easier for you, pursue it. Talk to your tutor, your parents, or anyone in a position to help you.

There are good applications available to ease studying. For example, if you're studying a difficult language, there are online resources and/or mobile applications that can help. Most of these have been specifically designed to make learning interesting. Some are free of charge. Explore them.

We are all aware of how the internet has revolutionised learning. YouTube has evolved to become a great learning resource. If a subject you're studying is difficult, or studying becomes arduous, turn to some tutorials on YouTube if you have access. Some students don't make very good use of their phones and laptops; don't be one of them.

Join a study group. Joining a study group can be very beneficial. What you find difficult may be easy for another student. Learning from other colleagues in a less tense environment can remove the seriousness of studies and make learning more fun. You have to be very careful of the study group you join though. If the group is large, your meetings are doomed to be less effective. If the members are 'parasites' (meaning they only want to learn from others), then it will not be very helpful. Choose/form study groups wisely.

Use what works for you. Before you start studying, select the time, environment, equipment, location, etc. that is best for you. If you prefer audios, record the lessons if you have a gadget to do so. If you prefer videos, look up online video material if you have the facilities to do so. If there is anything you can do to make studying less of a burden, do it. The easier studying becomes, the more likely you will keep doing it.

Help others. It has slowly come to my realisation that helping other students with their academic challenges can be of great benefit. It helps you gain deeper understanding of the topic you are helping the person with because, while teaching others, you learn as well. I remember a colleague of mine asked me for help with some questions on the eve of an exam. To my surprise, what I helped the person with was exactly what came up in the exam. It was more interesting to revise by helping my colleague than if I had revised on my own. I have to caution you to be very careful when you are helping others though. If you realise the person is becoming an unnecessary distraction, it is better to avoid that person if you can.

Summary

There is no success without hard work. Whether you are a biology student, music student, sports student, geography student, engineering student, architectural student, etc., hard work is a great catalyst for academic distinction.

Every hard worker must work smart as well. No matter how fast you run, if you run in the wrong direction, you will never get to your destination.

Reassessing your work should be an intrinsic part of your ethos as a hard-working student. It has made a big difference to my grades. As much as possible, make sure you reassess your assignments, course works, class tests, examination answers, essays, etc. As the Bible admonishes in Matthew 7:1, reassess your work and examine yourself.

Key 5: Get Some Attitude

Attitude is a little thing that makes a big difference.

Winston Churchill

The word *attitude* is sometimes (informally) used to refer to truculent or uncooperative behaviour. However, the actual meaning of attitude, according to the *Oxford Dictionary*, is 'a settled way of thinking or feeling about something'. As it is commonly said, your attitude will determine your altitude. *Altitude* here means your level of success. In this section, I am going to discuss some key attitudes you should possess as a student.

Be Disciplined

Mastering others is strength. Mastering yourself is
true power.

Lao Tzu

Discipline simply means training. I once heard someone say, 'A strong man is not someone who goes about beating everybody, but one who can beat himself.' Training oneself is one of the most difficult things to do but delivers great rewards. I believe this generation is one of the most undisciplined generations, where indiscipline has been nicknamed weakness. While some educational institutions are disciplining (training) students to achieve their greatest potential, unfortunately, others are shamefully allowing students to do whatever they want without challenging and training them adequately.

I would define discipline as doing what is required of you at the right time without listening to distractions from within (yourself) or externally. So, if you are supposed to be studying and you go 'Hmm, I think I need to sleep' or 'Hmm, let me go and have a chat' but defy that feeling and keep on studying, then you're disciplining (training) yourself. Giving in to your feelings is gross indiscipline. I am not talking about feeling sick or something that can physically prevent you from studying. I am talking about feelings that you can (and should) ignore.

When I was an undergraduate student, I usually had two weeks, uninterrupted by lectures, to prepare for exams. I spent nearly twelve hours revising every day during these periods. I had about three four-hour blocks and took intermittent breaks during these blocks. I had to train myself to do this. My body definitely didn't like it, but I knew what I wanted. I also knew that I did not have a photographic memory and had to revise again and again to retain things in my memory. I disciplined myself, and it paid big rewards. If you are a sports student, you have to discipline yourself to keep training and doing your exercises. If you are a music student, you have to discipline yourself to keep rehearsing and playing your instruments. If you are an art student, you have to discipline yourself and keep practising. No matter your field of study, you need to be disciplined to succeed.

Learning to defy feelings that can distract you can be challenging. Discipline is an attitude; it can be developed. You have to start where your strengths allow, and then you gradually challenge yourself to do what you couldn't do before. For example, if you usually play games for 2 hours when you are supposed to be studying, challenge yourself to study for 1 hour, and then play your game for 1 hour. If you master that, then you can move to 1.5 hours of study and thirty minutes of games. Finally, you can use the entire 2 hours to study.

Be Diligent

A person who is diligent in his works will stand before kings and not ordinary people (paraphrased).

Proverbs 22:29

Diligence is another attitude you need to develop. To be diligent as a student means to be careful in your studies. Most students do not appreciate the impact of being careful in their studies. You must not study just because you want to get a good job to feed yourself and your family in the future. You must study because you want to contribute significantly to the improvement of mankind. For this reason, we have to be careful to excel in our studies.

Some students are not diligent with some subjects or topics because they think they are irrelevant. The truth is, nothing is irrelevant. Take very good care to study whatever you are taught, and do your very best in it; you never know when the knowledge will be needed. At least be diligent in your studies so that you can pass your exams. Not everything I have learned in school has been directly beneficial in my job, but it has certainly broadened my knowledge.

Another aspect of diligence is doing well in whatever you need to do. Anything that is worth doing is worth doing well. Don't be sloppy or careless. Put in your best effort. When you do things to the best of your ability, it pays off. There is great regret in not doing your best when you're in school. I have a lot of friends who wish they could turn back the clock so they could do their best in school. This is a great heartache, and you don't want to experience it. Therefore, do the best you can with all you have, and you will not be disappointed. 'Whatever your hand finds to do, do it with all your might' (Ecclesiastes 9:10). I always advise students to do their best and forget the rest. Once you've put in your best, just hope for the best.

Be Determined

> The difference between the impossible and the possible lies in a man's determination.
>
> Tommy Lasorda

During the 2012 London Olympics, eyes all over the world were on the men's sprint. After winning the race, Usain Bolt was interviewed, and this is what he said:

> 'I was slightly worried about my start. I didn't want to false start again, so I think I sat in the blocks a little bit. I don't think it was the best reaction in the world but I executed, and that was the key . . . my coach said "stop worrying about the start, the best part of your race is the end; that's where you rule", so I stopped worrying about the past and I executed; so it worked.'

Apparently, Usain Bolt was disqualified in a previous race for false-starts so he was too careful with this race. Dwelling on the past slowed him down at the start of the race, but when he remembered the words of his coach — 'Stop worrying about the start, the best part of your race is the end' — he did just that, and he was the legendary winner.

Do you know that most people did not even notice he had a bad start in the race? Professional athletes would have recognized his bad start. Some people would have been totally oblivious to it, while others would have thought it was a strategy. No matter what it was to people, he won the race by refusing to worry and instead focusing on the future of the race. There are a few things we can learn from Usain's determination, and I want to share them with you.

Forget the past. The end of a thing is far more important than its beginning. How you end your student life is more important than how you started it. Those who hold on to the past have no hands to grab the future. We only look to the past to learn from it, not to live in it. Your past failures or successes belong to the past. Your ability to forget your past failures and focus on what is ahead is a powerful tool that can drastically change your future. You must learn not to dwell on past successes but forge ahead for future victories. I have had many students come to me for counselling about past failures, so I believe it is a big challenge to some students. I have been a victim of it as well. Previously I explained how I nearly failed a course because I answered it scientifically (from the wrong perspective).

Usually, one is tempted to think that a good beginning leads to a good end. This is not necessarily true. Overconfidence and complacency have robbed many of their possible successes. Some students start well but do not end well, while some students start well and end well. Some students do not start well but end well, while some students do not start well and do not end well. Your beginning can influence your end, but it is not the sole determinant of the end result — you are. You determine what the end result should be. Learn to forget the past.

Never give up. You should never ever give up; you must keep on keeping on. Usain Bolt had a valid reason to give up, but he didn't, and it paid off. Never give up on anything. It is better to give it your best shot, try and fail, than it is to give up. Whenever I feel like giving up in my academic pursuit, I tell myself, 'Giving up is a feeling, that's all it is. I have to bulldoze my way through the feeling.' Here are some tips to help you avoid giving up.

1. Redefine failure. In the Key 1 section, I specified how to define failure. If you refuse to see failure in an exam as a failure of your entire life, you will not be afraid to do your best in a course, assignment, or exam. Redefining failure will drive away fears.

2. Believe in yourself. Again, I mentioned in the Key 1 section that you are imbued with enormous potential to succeed. You need to believe in yourself. You will excel in your studies if you put your mind to it.

3. Be encouraged by others. Many students have been where you are and have succeeded. It is not because they are better than you are. If you keep doing the right things and practising the keys I've shared with you in this book, I believe you will make it.

Remember, quitters never win, and winners never quit. This is what Winston Churchill, one of Britain's highly acclaimed prime ministers, had to say to students:

'Never give in, never give in, never, never, never — in nothing, great or small, large or petty — never give in except to convictions of honour and good sense.'

Focus. The final lesson we learn from Usain's experience is focus. I'm sure you are aware of what concave lenses are. One popular experiment is to use them to focus the sun's rays on a small surface area. Depending on the intensity of the beam, it can produce a huge amount of energy to burn things. There is so much power in focus. Throughout my academic life, I have realised that students can dissipate their energies and attention on so many meaningless things that make them lose focus on what they're in school for. Sport is good, but if not taken in moderation – when your field of study is elsewhere – then it will make you lose focus. I understand some students may have to work to pay their fees, but this must be done in moderation also. Anything else that does not actively contribute to the success of your studies will have to be curtailed. Your time in school is your time for school. You have to focus all your energies into your education; focus is a key to success.

Be Daring

Do what you fear and fear disappears.

David J. Schwartz

Fear is a thief and a liar. It robs you of sound mind, and it makes you feel incapable. To the timid, fear means **f**orget **e**verything **a**nd **r**un, but to the bold fear means **f**ace **e**verything **a**nd **r**ise. It is commonly said that fear is false evidence appearing to be real. Fear is the strong, false sense of emotion that seems to overtake you when you're faced with a challenge. I know students who literally pass out when they're faced with a challenge (for example, examination).

When you fear, you lose ground, and you are unable to see the true picture of what you're faced with. Fear magnifies even the smallest challenge. Recall the job interview I mentioned earlier. At first glance, I nearly collapsed at the interview test for that job. I was so gripped by fear, I saw the questions as tough and complex. What made it worse was that I knew the company interviewing me was a reputable outfit seeking intellectuals and therefore would pose very difficult questions to sift out unsuitable candidates. I was left in the room to face this paper. After reading through the questions the first time, I was on the verge of giving up and running away. However, I did not want to disgrace myself, because I held a PhD. I sat quietly and decided to read the questions again. I read them over and over, until – just as a light bulb illuminates the darkness – I understood them. I found that I already knew the answers and thought to myself, *'Oh wow, how simple are these questions.'* I was really proud of myself that day. To be honest, the questions were very tricky but still simple.

Sometimes we're made to think courage is the absence of fear, but this is not always so. Even very experienced musicians sometimes get nerves when they get on the stage to perform. Having control over the nerves is how they can be overcome. As Nelson Mandela frankly put it, 'I learned that courage was not the absence of fear, but the triumph over it. The brave man is not he who does not feel afraid, but he who conquers that fear.'

Fear is just a feeling, and you have power and authority over it. Here are some ways to overcome fears in your studies.

1. Remember that yielding to fear is a choice. Yes, you may not consciously initiate it, but you choose to yield to it or feed it.

2. The more you feed fear, the less you feed courage, and vice versa. Feed courage through positive thinking.

3. Think of the worst that could happen. Most of the challenges we face in our academic lives do not have the ability to harm us, so why do we fear them? If you are a hill-climbing student and your exam is to jump off a one-hundred-metre cliff, then at least you have a legitimate cause for concern. However, I am very sure your examiner has everything in place to ensure your safety.

Be Discontented

> Let him who thinks he stands take
> heed lest he fall.
>
> 1 Corinthians 10:12

I am using the word *discontented* here to mean don't be complacent or overconfident. This section is for students who have been excelling. When you excel in a subject or make significant academic progress, be happy and content with your efforts. However, you must learn not to dwell on past glories. You must also remember there is more room for improvement.

I have coined the term *intelligent pitfalls* to represent some of the shortcomings well-performing (otherwise intelligent) students may fall into. From my observation, some intelligent students who do very well in lower educational levels experience a free fall in academic performance as they climb the academic ladder. I have come to the conclusion that some of these formally intelligent students may be committing one of many blunders: either they stopped working hard or they never cultivated the hard work attitude, or they got too complacent.

For any student, complacency may hit at various points. Here are some of the stages at which complacency may hit and the pitfalls to avoid:

1. *When you are moving from one academic level to another, say, from junior high to senior high.* Generally, as you climb the academic ladder, the subjects get more difficult. If you have a photographic memory, you may excel in high school, but your photographic memory may not be as helpful at university. To avoid this pitfall, always have an open mind, and be a bit inquisitive. Ask questions and seek understanding. Don't assume you know.

2. *When you underestimate new subjects you're not familiar with because you think they are similar to ones you have taken previously.* For example, a student thinking advanced mathematics is somewhat similar to the ordinary mathematics he or she is familiar with. To avoid this pitfall, have an open mind and be diligent with your

studies. Again, don't assume you know. Always ask your tutor for feedback.

3. *When you compare yourself with others and think you are better.* This is very dangerous. The fact that you are better than other students shouldn't get you overly excited. If, in an assignment, project, or exam you had the highest grade of 54 per cent, you will feel extremely satisfied when you compare yourself with your colleagues. However, you will quickly realise that your performance was very average when you compare yourself with the required standard of 100 per cent. To avoid this pitfall, always seek to meet the standard and not just to do better than others. Asking yourself how you could have done better can also help.

4. *Some students feel they are generally better than other students.* This is pride. The Bible admonishes us to consider others better than ourselves (Philippians 2:3). When colleagues come to you for help, help them, and don't look down on them. If you look down on others, how would you feel when they start performing better than you? Be humble and considerate.

Summary

Your attitude determines your altitude. Be disciplined and diligent in your studies. Resolve to never give up in your academic pursuits, because overcoming today's obstacles will lead you to tomorrow's successes. No matter how difficult things get, pursue your dream to the fullest.

Don't let fear rob you of your potential. Though you may have a fear of failure, don't let the feeling stop you from going higher. You have power to overcome fear; use it to your advantage. Finally, do not be overconfident. Overconfidence and complacency are pride. Pride comes before any fall. Be humble, be considerate, and have the hunger to learn more.

Key 6: Prepare for Exams

By failing to prepare, you are preparing to fail.

Benjamin Franklin

One of a meerkat's delicacies is scorpion. However, an encounter with such a delicacy is a real test, a test that can result in a nutritious meal or death. For this reason, baby meerkats (called pups) are trained by their parents to hunt this dangerous prey. When meerkats are born, their parents will go out and hunt food for them. However, as they grow up, the parents take them out and hunt prey in front of them. Later, the parents will ask them to kill the prey themselves or they will not eat. This is the sort of preparation a meerkat goes through before it can hunt a delicious but deadly scorpion.

The main aim of examinations and tests is not to fail students but, on the contrary, to improve them. However, those who are not well prepared for examinations usually fail them. Just like meerkats, students need to prepare adequately for tests, and they must start preparing early enough. It is a shame to know that most students think of exams as separate to the academic period. So, when a term or semester starts, these students wait until the exam period before they start preparations. This is a recipe for disaster. Just as meerkats have to prepare early on in life to tackle scorpions, you have to start preparing for exams from the beginning of the academic period.

In this section, I am going to give you some tips on how to prepare for and take examinations and tests.

Redefine Exams

> Examinations should be stepping stones, not stumbling blocks.
>
> Ernest Edifor

How would you define examinations? What does it mean to you? Unfortunately, most students fear exams, and some even pass out during exams. This should not be so. I know this may sound absurd: exam periods should be exciting times for students. It is a time for them to prove themselves. Sometimes students get apprehensive and nervous during exam periods, which is to be expected, but one must not be afraid. Yes, that's right!

Examinations should be stepping stones, not stumbling blocks. You must see examinations/tests as opportunities to show that you qualify to move to the next level of your academic pursuits. See exams and tests as good things; they are to help you progress. Don't be afraid of them. Prepare for them. I believe there is a direct relationship between students' preparedness for exams and their level of apprehension during exam periods. So, if you are well prepared for exams, you will be less afraid of them.

Don't disassociate your academic session from your exams. Most students think exams are the essays or tests they write at the end of an academic session and do not relate the session to the exams. Your academic session is to prepare you for your exams. The two are very much related. Therefore, if you don't take an academic session very seriously, you are bound to struggle in its exams.

Start Early

> It is better to read a little and thoroughly than cram
> a crude undigested mass into my head, though it be
> great in quantity.
>
>   Thomas Huxley

Some students wait until it is time for a test or exam before they start preparing. This leads to what is called cramming, mugging or swotting. Cramming is the process of committing huge volumes of information to memory within a short period, usually in preparation for exams. Cramming is not recommended; it should be a student's last option.

An excellent way to avoid cramming is to start studying for exams earlier on in the academic session. Many (if not all) students desire to excel in exams, but not many prepare adequately for them. Preparation for exams should start right from the beginning of the academic term, semester or trimester. When you start early, you put less pressure on yourself, you build more confidence in yourself, and you are less afraid of exams. Start early to avoid rushing at the end. Other ways to avoid cramming are to practise the keys described earlier in this book. Avoid procrastination, break your tasks into chunks, work hard, plan your time, study smarter, be disciplined and diligent, improve your memory, avoid distractions, solve past questions, etc. If you are able to practise these from the start of your academic session, you will avoid the need to cram and have good success. Preparing for exams should not start during exams periods; it should start when tuition starts.

Learn in Class

> I never learn anything talking. I only learn things
> when I ask questions.
>
> Lou Holtz

I know and understand that there are different modes of learning, and that students learn differently. Unfortunately, due to lack of sufficient resources in most educational institutions, students are compelled to all learn in class the same way. The traditional mode of learning in class is to sit with other students while you listen to a lecture or demonstration by a tutor or lecturer.

Though this may not be the preferred mode of learning for most students, it is the prevailing situation. To make the most of this, I encourage all students to learn in class. Make sure you understand what the tutor is teaching. To do so:

1. ask questions for clarifications when necessary
2. avoid distractions
3. take short breaks (use the toilet) if the lesson is too long for you.
4. concentrate; if you lose concentration, try to catch up
5. take notes and jot down salient points.

After learning in class, make sure you revise. That is, look over what has been taught and practise ample exercises on it. I always advise students to revise what they have been taught on the same day if possible. When you are able to learn in class and revise adequately afterwards, you will be prepared for exams.

Examination Tips

Below are some helpful tips on things to do/not do before, during, and after exams.

Before Exams

Avoid distraction. I have already spoken about avoiding distractions. Because I have been a victim of this, I want to warn you again on distractions: avoid them. Always endeavour to plan your studies so that you don't lose concentration.

Take mock tests. Take as many mock tests as possible. You can time yourself on some past questions. Solve as many past questions as you can lay your hands on. If past questions are not available, create questions for yourself. Some teachers will not mind giving you mock questions; just ask. You can also try solving some past questions from other schools/colleges other than yours if the topics are very similar.

Revise. It is common sense that you need to revise before exams. Go over your notes as many times as possible. Remember that the scope of coverage is not as important as the depth. So, you don't have to cover every topic you've been taught, but you need to know what you have covered very well. If you read one hundred pages of your notes but cannot remember anything, then the student who read only one page and can remember it has a better chance of success.

Watch your health. Make sure you're eating, sleeping, and drinking well. Sleep well or sleep moderately. Eight hours of sleep is recommended. Eat foods that can boost your memory and general well-being. Avoid highly processed foods and foods with artificial sweeteners. Drink a lot of water and healthy fruit juices if you can.

During Exams

Prioritise your work. Apart from multiple-choice questions, it is recommended that you skim through the questions first. As you do so, identify questions you think you can tackle. Answer the questions in order of difficulty. You don't need to skim through multiple-choice questions before answering them; some can have up to a hundred questions. Answer multiple-choice questions as you read them. Mark out difficult ones or those requiring more effort and return to them later on. Also, be sure to select questions with higher marks. You can use the steps below as a guide in prioritising exam questions:

1. easy questions with higher marks
2. easy questions with lower marks
3. difficult questions with higher marks
4. difficult questions with lower marks

Do not spend too much time prioritising the exam questions. You only need to spend the first few minutes doing so. Practise these steps during the mock exams you set for yourself so that you can master them before the actual exams.

Organize yourself. After selecting and prioritising your work, assign times to each question. Always make sure to have a watch with you in the exam hall if you can, and it is allowed. When the time allocated to a question is over and you haven't finished answering it, you can go ahead, if you feel you can finish it. However, if you cannot answer a question and the time allocated to it has been exhausted, move on to another question.

Divide and conquer. Always use the chunking method. Divide big or difficult questions into smaller, manageable chunks. Don't ever be afraid of exam questions; they are easier to tackle when divided. Sometimes you may have to think carefully about how to divide questions into chunks. It works wonders.

Reassess your work. When you have answered all questions and if you have spare time, always, always review your work. Reassessing your work usually reveals errors. When reassessing your work, put yourself in the examiner's shoes.

Avoid Cheating. Never cheat during exams. Cheating puts you in danger of wasting all the effort you have put into your course. Not only will you face punishment and jeopardize your future, but you could also be hurting the people you care about and those who support you.

Recover. Finally, if you go blank during an exam, do your best to recover immediately. Different techniques work for different people. You may want to put your head on the desk for few minutes, use the toilet if possible, take deep breaths, etc.

After Exams

Rest and prepare. After an exam, if you have other exams pending, you should rest and prepare for the other exams. Don't waste the time, even if you have two weeks or more before the next exam. Revise and avoid distractions from friends, social media, etc.

Reward yourself. After exams, reward yourself. Give yourself a good treat if you are able to do so.

Summary

Examinations are not to be feared or hated by students; they are supposed to be good things. They facilitate promotion and advancement. Ill-prepared students fear exams.

Preparation for exams is a vital key to success in academia. Preparation for exams shouldn't start a few weeks prior to the exams but should start at the beginning of the course. Applying the other keys described in this book can help you prepare adequately for your exams.

Key 7: Read, Read, Read

There are many little ways to enlarge your child's world. Love of books is the best of all.

Jacqueline K. Onassis

In the 1950s, a young boy living in Detroit, USA, performed very poorly in school and had a horrible temper. His mother, who single-handedly raised him and his brother, was unfortunately a third-grade school leaver. However, this woman did not want her children to end up like her, so she wisely decided to take action. Her sons would no longer watch so much television, so she enrolled them in the local library.

Reading generated curiosity in this young boy and helped build his imagination. Straight away he started doing very well in school. His grades started improving, and before he knew it, he was the best student in his class. The simple, ruthless step his mother took transformed him from a poor-performing student to the best-performing student.

He grew up to attend some of the prestigious medical schools in America and became the first neurosurgeon to perform a successful separation of conjoined twins. He went on to perform many other medical operations that have saved so many lives and brought happiness to many families. He has a scholarship fund supporting thousands of needy students across America. He has authored bestselling books and has received many awards for his tremendous contributions. This is the story of the legendary Dr. Ben Carson. His story gives me a lot of inspiration.

Reading, they say, makes a full man. Reading is wonderful. Reading can change your life; it changed Ben Carson's life. I am not talking about reading your textbooks or notebooks here, I am talking about reading in general. I am talking about reading literature (books, articles, posts, etc.) on history, nature, fiction, autobiographies, etc. There are several benefits you can derive from reading. Reading is a good exercise for your brain and memory, and helps you build imagination; it improves your critical thinking skills, focus and concentration. It is unarguable that reading helps you build your vocabulary, improves your grammar and enhances your writing skills. Reading gives you knowledge, and knowledge is power. Reading can provide you with calmness and stress relief. There is no substitute for reading; you can listen to audios or watch videos, but they will not be able to deliver all the benefits you can derive from reading. Reading is powerful!

In this section, I am going to give you some tips on how you can improve your reading skills and become an avid reader (if you are not already one).

Find Your Interest

> The very first step towards success in any occupation is to become interested in it.
>
> William Osler

To succeed in any field of endeavour, you need some level of interest. To build your interest in reading, you will have to select books in your area of interest. I love books on motivation, general science and invention. History is not my thing. Neither is romance. You may be different. If you pick books you are interested in, you are more likely to read them to completion. Conversely, if you read books that do not particularly interest you, you are more likely to quit.

You have to locate a source that will give you your literature of interest. You can use a local library, as Ben Carson's mother did. You can also ask friends or relations. I have borrowed books from friends and lent to others. Sharing is a great way to get access to books. You may also want to join a book club or form one if you are interested in doing so. As you get your pocket money, you may want to save some for books. I have personally bought books that have greatly helped me. Another great source of reading materials is the internet. There are free books, articles and other literature available for your consumption online. If you have internet access, I would encourage you to explore this avenue.

Sometimes, it helps to get a mentor or someone involved in your field of interest. This person could be your parents, a tutor, a family relative, a librarian, etc. They will challenge you and guide you in your reading pursuits. If you don't have someone like that, you may have to get a friend who is also willing to read, and both of you can share experiences. If you don't have such a friend, you will have to encourage yourself. Encouraging yourself can be challenging, but if you stick to reading books that interest you, you will make it a lot easier. Always look for literature of interest to you; it makes all the difference.

Find Time

> I never need to find time to read . . . I read when
> I'm drying my hair. I read in the bath. I read when
> I'm sitting in the bathroom. Pretty much anywhere
> I can do the job one-handed, I read.
>
>   Joanne K. Rowling

One of the big excuses people have for not reading is lack of spare time. I don't think this is true. I think the more appropriate answer would be lack of interest. We can always make time for what we are interested in. If you want to encourage a reading culture, you will undoubtedly have to make time to read.

My sister, Regina, who has climbed the academic ladder (from a very humble beginning) through prestigious international scholarships and ended up at Yale, was an avid reader. She read almost any time and anywhere. The most absurd was in the kitchen when she stirred food on the cooker with one hand and read a book with the other. She devoured any piece of literature she found interesting. She is such an inspiration.

My life took a different turn when I started reading. I used every avenue available to pick a book to read. I read when I was on the bus. I read early in the morning and late at night. I read when classes were cancelled. I read while I was waiting to be attended to in the hospital or in a queue. I read whenever I had spare time. I read almost everywhere, and you can do the same too. You can make time if you plan your day. You can always use spare time reading.

Visualize and Imagine

> Imagination is more important than knowledge.
>
> Albert Einstein

What you see when you read is very important. I am not talking about what you see with your physical eyes but what you see in your mind's eyes; what you visualize. When you read, endeavour to see whatever you're reading in your mind's eye. Imagination is what brings reading to life. Here are some of the benefits of visualization or imagination:

1. You gain more understanding. Building a mental picture or story of what you read usually gives you deeper

understanding of what you're reading and also helps you relate what you are reading to what you have previously read, and what you will be reading in the future.

2. Imagination also improves your memory. Earlier, I spoke of improving your memory by association. Imagination is a big part of association. When you can imagine things, you can easily recollect them.

3. Imagination goes hand –in-hand with invention. A wonderful thing about imagination is that it can be changed/modified without any consequences. If you can imagine things you read, you can modify them, and this can lead to invention.

When you read, try to see what you read in your mind's eye. It will be beneficial in most (if not all) of your fields of endeavour.

Keep Reading

> Anyone who stops learning is old, whether at twenty or eighty. Anyone who keeps learning stays young. The greatest thing in life is to keep your mind young.
>
> Henry Ford

Many people fall into the habit of reading less as they grow older. I have experienced this and would not recommend it. Read until it is a habit, and when it becomes a habit, keep reading. In order to keep reading, you have to employ some of the keys I have mentioned in this book:

1. Plan to read and use any spare time for reading, or your spare time will usually be taken up by something else.
2. You have to work on your reading. Don't let feelings of indolence rob you of reading time.
3. You have to be determined, disciplined and diligent in your reading.
4. Get a reading partner, join a reading club, or have a mentor who will challenge you to read.

Summary

Good writers are usually good readers. Since you will be required to write a lot in your academic endeavours, it is beneficial to cultivate a reading habit. There are several benefits to reading. Reading transformed the life of a low-performing student into a world-renowned doctor who has saved many lives. Read, read and read.

A Message to Parents

> Your children need your presence more than your presents.

> Jesse Jackson

One thing a child needs most from a parent is the parent. Your child needs your presence more than your presents. Working hard to provide for a child is great, but you have to be careful you don't rob that child of you. The best way you can express love for your child is to spend time with them. Spend time listening to them, spend time helping them with their homework, spend time playing with them, spend time chatting with them, spend time reading them stories, spend time watching cartoons with them, spend time taking them out, spend time with them.

If you don't spend time with your child, your child will spend his/her time with something/someone else. If whatever your child spends his/her time with does not make a positive influence in his/her life you are in danger of losing your child in the future. Frederick Douglass rightly said, 'It is easier to build strong children than to repair broken men.'

One of the greatest investments a parent can give to a child is to spend time with them. This is sometimes difficult to do, but every parent must make sacrifices to do this if they love their children.

A Message to Teachers

The mediocre teacher tells. The good teacher explains. The superior teacher demonstrates. The great teacher inspires.

William Arthur Ward

A teacher's role is more than transferring information/facts to students. A teacher is supposed to be a student's mentor or inspirer. A teacher's job is to introduce his/her pupils or students to topics, courses, and to challenge them, mentor them and inspire them to explore and make good use of what they have been taught.

Students are different and they learn differently. It is the duty of a teacher to empower each student so that they can discover themselves and make most use of their talents and abilities. Albert Einstein said, 'Everybody is a genius, but if you judge a fish by its ability to climb a tree it will live its whole life believing that it is stupid.' One of the biggest mistakes a teacher can make is to force students into becoming what they are not. However, a teacher's greatest joy is to see his/her students fulfilling their purpose and advancing the course of humanity.

As a teacher, you have a great responsibility; the world is depending on you to train the future leaders in your care. Please fulfil your duties with all diligence.